THE SUPADUPA KID 2

written by

TY ALLAN JACKSON

illustrated by

JONATHAN SHEARS

D0723978

Published by Big Head Books

© 2019 by Tyrone Allan Jackson

All rights reserved. No part of this publication may be reproduced or transmitted in any shape or by any means, electronic, mechanical, photocopying, recording or otherwise, without prior written permission of Big Head Books.

Library of Congress Control Number
2020910538

ISBN: 978-0-578-70686-3

Printed in the U.S.A.

This book is dedicated to every student, educator, administrator, cafeteria worker and custodian, in every elementary school across the country!

But particularly to Brooke Burnett, Dr. Esch and everyone at Beverly J. Martin Elementary School in Ithaca, N.Y.

You are all SUPADUPA ;)

The Supadupa Kid 2 - MOVE

By Ty Allan Jackson

The Supadupa Kid 2: MOVE

I have to admit, I kinda like this superhero thing!

What could be more awesome than having superpowers? I can shoot lightning bolts outta my hands. KABOOM! I can fly. SWOOSH! And all the girls think my outfit is really cute! Okay... maybe not all the girls.

To top it all off, I've got the most awesome sidekick ever. Ronald isn't just my main bro, he's arguably the smartest kid on the planet. Without him, there would be no way I would have defeated Hoody, my arch-enemy from school last year. And with Hoody out of the picture, I can just kinda chill.

Crime here in Littletown, New York, is the lowest it's been in decades because all the bad guys know they're going to get their butts kicked if they try to dirty up my city. Even Mayor Malley said..."The City of Littleton owes The Supadupa Kid a tremendous amount of gratitude for making our streets safe again."

And with the street safe from criminals, and no villains with powers like mine tearing the city apart, I can just be a normal kid...or so I thought.

1

Maya Gonzalez is witty, tough, really smart and not to mention, really pretty.

Maya's family moved here from Mexico a few years ago. When she came to Booker T. Washington Middle School, she barely spoke a word of English. But in less than three years of living in The United States, not only did she learn the language, she quickly rose up the ranks to become one of the smartest students in the school. She ranks at the top in every class except science. There's no way BrainBoy Ronald is letting anyone steal that title from him. That nut named his hamsters Bunsen and Burner. I mean, come on, Ronald. Anyway...

It took me a little while to get up the nerve to say hello to Maya, but when I did I was pretty smooth. After some coaching from our Spanish teacher, Señora Montalvo, I knew just how to roll up on her.

It was lunch time, and she was sitting all alone at a table near the back of the cafeteria. Ronald was nudging me along to go and say something.

"Come on, SDK!" Ronald coaxed.

"Don't call me that in public," I replied sternly.

"FINE! If you don't go and say hi to her, then I will."

"OK, OK...I'm going."

I knew what I was going to say, and I was going to be smooth saying it. Yeah, the smoothest guy in Booker T. Middle School, that's me.

So I tossed a breath mint in my mouth, checked my hair in Ronald's extra thick glasses, which was easy to do because the lenses are about the size of two small planets and glided over to her table.

Just as I was ready to make my move, Donald Rumpt, the biggest bozo in the school, slapped the tray of food I was holding straight up in the air. Peas, carrots, milk, and the world's worst meatloaf flew everywhere. The milk fell on me first and splashed all over my brand new sneakers, which, despite being brand new, have zero traction. I took one step to avoid the onslaught of food, slipped on the spilled milk and fell flat on my butt.

"OW!"

As I lay pathetically on the floor, vegetables bombarded me like green and orange bullets falling from the sky. Then the meatloaf (A.K.A. Deathloaf) fell directly into my mouth as I screamed and almost choked to death. "AGGGGGGGGG!"

Of course this caught the attention of the entire 8th grade. Everyone burst out laughing at my downfall, even my best bud, Ronald! Traitor. For about 10 seconds I felt like the biggest loser in school, until I heard the most angelic voice in the world.

"Are you okay?" Maya asked softly, as she took a napkin and wiped the milk away from my brow.

"Oh, yeah! I'm cool. This isn't the first time a school lunch almost killed me. I'm just glad it wasn't the chicken. There's no way I would've survived the golden nuggets of doom."

"Tee-hee," she chuckled.

She grabbed a few more napkins, took the peas and carrots out of my hair, and wiped the gravy off my face. I must have looked like a used barf bag. Thank goodness cell phones aren't allowed in school, because I'm sure a video of the peas and carrots meteor shower would have gotten a gazillion hits on Youtube. I don't mind going viral saving the city, but not as a bowl of succotash.

After Maya was kind enough to make me look human again, she invited me to sit with her and share her lunch.

"*Siéntate,*" she said softly.

"What?"

"Please sit down."

"Oh...sure...thanks."

Here was my chance to WOW her with my extremely limited Spanish. "*Muchas gracias,* Maya."

"OH! De nada, Javon."

"Hey! You know my name."

"*Sí.* Of course I know your name. You're in my class and the teacher seems to call on you more than anyone else. You're obviously very popular and smart."

"I guess you could say that," I said with a sly smirk on my face.

All of a sudden I could feel Ronald's breath, which smelled like a bucket of wet pencils, breathing down my neck.

"Hola, mi nombre es Ronald. Cómo está usted?"

I sneered at Ronald and whispered in his ear, "Show off."

"AH! Mi nombre es Maya, muy bien Señor Ronald."

BrainBoy was grinning from ear to ear.

"It's nice to meet you, Ronald. You're known as the smartest kid in school, and the fact that you can speak Spanish so well is pretty awesome!"

"Aww shucks, Maya," he said beamingly.

RINGGGGGGGGG!

"Oh well," Ronald said, "Looks like lunch is over. I'm so excited to get back to science class. Mr. Sykes said he got new microscopes for our class projects. WOO-HOO!"

"Oh, brother," I said, rolling my eyes. "Maya, do you mind if I walk you back to class?"

"That's really sweet of you, Javon," Maya said while she flipped her hair. It was just like in the movies. All slow motion like! It's like time stood still. SWOON! I just melted until pencil-breath Ronald said:

"Hey, Javon, mind if I walk with you guys?" Ronald shouted.

Grrrrrr! I mumbled under my breath.

2

Meet the Thomas Triplets: Tracy, Tanya, and Tammy.

These three young ladies have brought fear into the hearts of every student in this school...and a few teachers. By the looks of them you'd think they were perfectly harmless, cute even. They look like bronzed-skinned Barbie dolls, but act more like Chucky from the slasher flicks. Their baby faces create this amazing illusion that they can be trusted, and even admired. But make no mistake, The Treacherous Three (A.K.A. the T3) is a three-headed monster built to cause havoc and pain.

Tracy is the leader of the three. She can make a girl cry just by staring into her eyes. She seems to hypnotize people and make them crumble with just a glance. Tracy is so mean, she once called the police on a kid's lemonade stand because he didn't have a permit to sell beverages! Luckily for the kid, the cops showed him how to get a permit and even bought a cup! I think the kid's name was Danny?

Then there's Tammy, who has the voice of a banshee! I swear she can break glass with her high-pitched screech. And when she laughs, I'm pretty sure she's communicating with hyenas somewhere in Africa!

Last, and definitely least, is Tanya, who is as smart as a basketball. She rarely speaks, but when she does it usually starts with, "DUH..."

Despite being triplets, they are not identical. They all look and act kind of different, except for their clothes. They wear the exact same outfit everyday! WHO DOES THAT!? And they wear different, colored hair bands.

Tracy wears pink.

Tanya wears yellow.

Tammy wears purple.

Sadly, everyone knows this because when they introduce themselves they'll say: "Hi, I'm Tracy 'Pink' Thomas" and "I'm Tanya 'Yellow' Thomas"...you get the picture.

The three of them sit next to each other in every class. Whenever one of them does something they think is cool, clever or funny, they simultaneously snap their fingers. REALLY LOUDLY! I don't know how they're capable of doing it so loud or how they always do it in sync. It's kinda scary. It's more like they're clones than triplets.

After the meatloaf fiasco, we were sitting in science class, which is of course Brainboy's favorite class, and Mr. Sykes asked, "Who can tell me the difference between a proton and a neutron?"

"Ooooh! I can tell you, Mr. Sykes. A proton..."

"NO! Not you, Ronald. Let's give someone else a chance."

"Fine!" Ronald pouted.

"How about you, Tracy?"

"WELL...Both protons and neutrons are present in the nucleus of an atom, but a proton is positively charged, and a neutron is neutral."

The three SNAPPED in unison.

"That is correct, Tracy. Well done."

SNAP!

"UGH! That is so annoying!" said Maya.

"Nobody asked you," the Treacherous Three said, all together.

"And how does an electron come into play, Maya?" asked Mr. Sykes.

"Unlike a proton, an electron is negatively charged and is spread around the nucleus," Maya boasted, as she turned around to smirk at the triplets.

"WHATEVER," sneered the three... IN UNISON!!! Seriously, how do they do that!?

"I knew that," Ronald shouted out proudly.

"Okay, class. Tomorrow we're going to focus on the science of sound and the power of vibration."

RIIIIIIIING!

"Nice job, everyone. Have a great day!" said Mr. Sykes.

"Hey, Maya, wait up! What are you doing after school?" I asked, trying to play it cool.

"I have a big math test tomorrow, and I really need to study. But I'm free on Sunday if you'd like to do something, Javon."

There's something about the way she says my name that makes me want to fly, literally.

"Sure, Maya. Sunday it is. Have a great day, and good luck on your math test tomorrow."

I waved goodbye and turned to go to my next class.

"HEY!" Ronald shouted, bumping into me so hard I shot a lightning bolt on to the floor! Fortunately no one noticed.

"DUDE!"

"So, what's up with Señorita Cutie Pie?!" Ronald inquired, winking.

"Haha! Ronald, you're too funny. Looks like I'm taking her out on Sunday."

"UP TOP!"

As we high-fived, I accidentally shocked Ronald, and he yelped out, "OUCH!"

"Oops...Sorry, bro! Maybe you can invent something to minimize the shock?"

"Maybe instead you can stop treating me like I'm a microwaveable dinner. That really stings," Ronald said, blowing on his finger tips.

"So, where are you going to take her?"

"I don't know! Maybe CrazyWorld? "

We both looked at each other and said, "NAH!"

3

Unlike most of the students at school, who get picked up by their parents or take the yellow bus, Maya walks home. Maya's family believes in hard work and self-reliance, and considering Maya only lives a mile away, walking is a piece of cake.

It takes Maya about 30 minutes to walk home if she takes Main Street, but if she goes behind the school, there's a path that cuts about 15 minutes off her time. The path goes through a pretty woodsy area in the beginning, and after about 10 minutes there is a big clearing called the Bald Spot. A lot of kids play softball or soccer at the Bald Spot. It's also the place where a few gangs will come to hang after hours.

On this particular day, Maya wanted to get an early start studying, so she took the path. She walked with her younger sister, María, who is in the 2nd grade and loves school. Anything having to do with school makes María happy. From the pledge of allegiance to the final bell, and everything in between, school puts a smile on María's face.

"Maya! HOW! WAS! YOUR! DAY!?" María joyfully shouted out while skipping.

"It was pretty good, Sis. This cute boy named Javon asked me to go out with him on a date Sunday."

"Ooooh! Are you gonna kiss him?"

"What?! NO! I think you're watching too many soap operas with Mamà. He's just really nice. Unlike those awful triplets. They are so mean!"

"What did they do, Maya?" Marìa asked, concerned.

"YEAH! What did we do?!" Tracy screeched as she pushed Maya from behind.

When Marìa and Maya turned around, The Treacherous Three were standing behind them, arms crossed, with the smuggest looks on their faces.

"WE DON'T LIKE YOU!" they all said in unison.

"How do you do that?" Maya asked.

"DO WHAT?" they all yelled.

"Never mind. Well, I don't like you either," Maya said sternly.

"Oh, yeah?!" Tammy yelled, then pushed Maya into Tanya.

"Oh, yeah?!" As Tanya pushed Maya into Tracy.

"OH, YEAH?!" Tracy pushed Maya onto the ground. Maya fell and bumped her head on a rock, bruising her temple.

"MAYA!" Marìa yelled.

"Oops! You shouldn't be so clumsy, Maya!" Tracy taunted.

As the girls snickered, Tracy grabbed Marìa by the shirt and said, "If you whisper one word of this to ANYONE, you'll regret it! Understand?"

Marìa nodded her head as Tracy pushed her down toward her sister.

The three skipped away while twirling their hair and giggling.

"Maya! Are you okay!?"

"I'm fine, Marìa, are you?" asked Maya as she dusted the dirt off her brightly colored skirt.

"I'm okay," said Marìa.

"OUCH!" Maya yelped, as she touched the newly formed bump on her head. "I guess I'll be wearing a hat for the next few days."

4

"Hey, Dad! What's for dinner?" I yelled, busting into the house at top speed before realizing I made a big mistake!

"I mean, hey Dad, how was your day?"

My dad is all about respect. We greet each other kindly in this family. Although it pains me to be nice to my little sister Denise, I do it because if I don't and Dad catches me, he'll make me clean the garage or worse, under my bed!

"Great recovery, son. My day was good. Being the local TV weather man is kinda like being a punching bag or a teddy bear. When the weather is bad, the public beats me up. Like I control the weather," he said, rolling his eyes. "When the weather is beautiful, like today, everyone wants to hug me like a teddy bear. And to answer your original question, we're having spaghetti for dinner. Your mother performed a complicated surgical procedure today, so I want to make sure dinner is perfect. Would you mind making the salad and setting the table, Javon? Your mother and sister should be home any moment."

"Of course, Dad! The men of the house got this!" As I gave Dad a high five, a spark shot out of my fingertips and shocked him.

"WOW-WEE! What in the world was that?! You shocked the hair off my head!"

"Dad, you're already bald!"

"Exactly!"

We both had a big laugh and finished preparing dinner.

After dinner, I helped Denise with her science homework. She doesn't usually ask me for help, so she must have really needed it. I love being a big brother, even though she doesn't make it easy! Last week she put gum in my hair. The week before she put shaving cream in my sneakers, and just yesterday she put olive oil on my toilet seat. When I woke up and went to the bathroom to do my business, I sat down on the toilet and slid to the floor! I could hear her outside laughing her butt off while my butt was on the floor, all greasy. I can't stand her and love her at the same time.

"Thanks for helping me, big brother," Denise said sweetly. I immediately looked up, thinking that something was going to fall on my head. Then I looked around, waiting for some catastrophe, but everything seemed okay, which made me even more nervous.

"What are you looking for, Javon?" she asked.

"I'm looking for your usual prank. I know you're up to something, Denise." "Not this time. I can be nice every once in a while."

"Cool! Thanks, Denise. You're not so bad after all. Good luck on your test tomorrow." As I walked out of her bedroom, I didn't notice the string at the bottom of the door. I tripped over the string and landed on my butt. The string was connected to a bag of flour that was above the door and fell directly on my head.

POOF!

I looked like a dusty ghost.

Denise was cackling like a hen!

"MOM!" I screamed, while spitting the chalky flour outta my mouth.

Mom and Dad ran upstairs, only to see me on the floor, looking like a piece of chicken before going into the fryer.

Next thing you know, we were all laughing at the top of our lungs. I really love my family. Even Denise...sometimes.

After a one-hour shower to get all the flour out of places I don't want to mention, I went into my room to play video games.

5

"Maya, are you okay?"

"Yes, Mamà, I just fell and bumped my head on the walk home. I'm fine."

"Oh, let me get some ice for your head."

Maya looked down at Marìa and mimed a *Shhhh!*

Marìa nodded her head.

"Maya, here's an ice pack."

"Ow!" Maya yelped as Mamà gently placed the ice pack on a bump as big as a golf ball.

"Now go and lie down for a little while. I'm making a huge dinner!"

"Why, Mamà?"

"We're having Nana Hilda come stay with us for a little while."

"YAY!" Maya yelled, which was immediately followed by an, "OUCH!"

"Okay, Mamà. I'm going to lie down. I can't wait to see Nana Hilda. I love her."

"Me too. She's coming all the way from Mexico to spend some time with us. I'm so excited. Marìa, why don't you go with Papà to pick her up from the airport?"

"*Sí, Mamà.*"

Two hours later, when Maya woke up from her nap, Nana Hilda was lying beside her.

Nana Hilda was full of such wisdom. You could see it on her face, and feel it when she touched you with her hands. Culture, history, wisdom, and love were all wrapped up in Nana Hilda.

"Oh, my Maya. You've gotten so big since I last saw you. You look so beautiful. Just like your mother when she was your age. Mija, what happened to your head?"

"*Hola,* Nana. It's good to see you, too. I've missed you so much. Oh, my head? It's just a little bump," Maya said.

"How did you get this bump?" Nana Hilda asked knowingly.

"Ummm, I fell."

"Really?"

"*Sí,* Nana...really."

Of course, wise Nana Hilda knew that something was not right.

6

The next day in science class, Mr. Sykes asked Maya about the bump on her head.

"Maya, are you okay? What happened to your head?"

"Yes, Mr. Sykes. I'm fine. I fell," Maya said as she shied away from Mr. Sykes' glance.

"Very well, Maya. Can you tell me what this is?" He held up a weird-looking steel item that looked like a two-pronged fork.

"It's a tuning fork. My Papà uses it to balance sound when he's tuning his guitar."

"That's correct, Maya, nice job. A tuning fork is used to tune and balance all types of instruments, including the human voice, which is also an instrument. I want everyone to hold up the tuning fork that I placed on the desk in front of you and give it a little tap. Feel the power coming from it. When you tap the fork, it changes the molecules in the air and creates the sound and vibration you're feeling now. Feels cool, right, students?" Mr. Sykes asked proudly.

"It's good to see that bump didn't make you dopey, Maya," Tanya said, as she and her sisters snickered.

You could see Maya seething with anger.

After class was over, I went up to Maya. "Hey, are we still on for Sunday? If your head hurts we could wait," I said, hoping she wouldn't cancel on me.

"No, Javon. I'm looking forward to it!"

"Sweet!"

"Did you say 'sweets', Javon?" Ronald shouted.

"HAHA, Ronald, you're too much."

Unfortunately the Treacherous Three were listening in on our conversation. "Look at the three little dorks," Tracy said with her hands on her hips.

"I bet none of them have a date for the big dance next week!" Tanya said.

"Maybe they can all go together!" the three said in unison.

"Maybe they can wear matching outfits like us!"

"HAHAHAHAHA!"

"You three are such losers!" Maya said angrily.

"LOSERS?!" The triplets all said together.

"Yeah...LOSERS! Which rhymes with schmoozer, which you should be very familiar with, because if your rich parents didn't schmooze with Principal Johnson and give a big donation to the school, you would all be failing every single class!"

I gasped. Ronald gasped. And unfortunately for Maya, Principal Johnson was standing right behind Maya and gasped.

"Is that so, Maya? To my office right this moment!" Principal Johnson said harshly.

"Yes, sir!" Maya said, blushing.

As Maya turned to walk away, Tracy stuck out her little designer shoe and tripped Maya!

"AHHHH!" Maya screamed as she fell on the hard tiled floor and hit her knee. The triplets gingerly walked away, and of course, Principal Johnson didn't see a thing.

Ronald and I helped Maya up and she limped to the principal's office.

7

"Maya, I have to admit I am very disappointed in you," Mamà scolded that evening. "Tell your Papà and Nana what happened, then you can take your dinner into your room and think about what you did."

"But, Mamà...it wasn't my fault, really!" Maya pleaded.

"Did you accuse Principal Johnson of giving those Thomas girls good grades unjustly?"

"Yes, Mamà," Maya said sadly.

"Then it is your fault! Accept responsibility and go to your room!"

Frustrated, Maya slumped out of her chair and did the slow walk of shame to her bedroom.

A few minutes later, Nana Hilda came into Maya's room.

"Are you okay, *Mija*?"

"Yeah, I mean yes, Nana Hilda. I'm fine."

"I don't think you're fine at all. I know what is going on, Maya. There is a girl bullying you in school, right?"

"How did you know, Nana?"

"I have my ways," Nana winked. "In fact, I can tell it's more than one, isn't it? There is a number and a letter sticking in my head. T and 3. Tell me, Maya, what does that mean?"

"How did you know that, Nana?" Maya inquired again. "Nana has her ways," she said with a smile.

"There are triplets whose names all start with T, and they hate me. They gave me this bump on my head and made me hurt my knee today."

"When I was your age, I had a similar issue, but it was with only one girl, not three. Her name was Esmerelda. To look at her, you would think she was kind, but she was pure evil. No one would believe it when I told them all the bad things she did to me. She would punch me, kick me, and she even pulled out my hair. She always said it was an accident, and everyone believed her. Except my own nana. She knew the same way I knew that someone was hurting you. When I saw my nana the day after some particularly nasty bullying, she gave me something. Something very special, very sacred. Something I am going to give to you now, but understand that there is magic in this gift. It has the power to help you in ways you can't imagine, but it also has the power to do things that cannot be undone."

Maya listened to her grandmother eagerly.

Nana Hilda continued, "Maya, our family has an amazing legacy of kings, queens and warriors. You are the descendant of one of the most powerful tribes in the Maya Civilization, which is why your mother named you Maya. Your ancestors could do things that people control the weather, communicate with animals, and even move objects just by thinking about them."

"What are you talking about, Nana?"

Maya asked skeptically.

Nana Hilda was wearing a strange necklace. The chain was a leather rope. It looked worn and weathered but strong and durable. She took it from around her neck and revealed an amulet. It was so beautiful. Only about the size of a quarter, but it was the most amazing shade of crimson red.

Nana Hilda put the necklace around Maya's neck, placing one hand on her forehead, and the other on the amulet. Maya thought that something dramatic would happen, but the necklace just felt kinda cold. Then Nana Hilda began to chant.

"Ahora tienes el poder."

"Ahora tienes el poder."

"Ahora tienes el poder."

Maya instantly felt tired. Her eyes became heavy and her mind became foggy.

"Sleep well, my Mija, for when you awaken, the first word to come out of your mouth will be your gift. Sleep... sleep...sleep."

"YAWN...Nana, you're bugging out! I don't believe in this hocus pocus, mumbo jumbo...YAWN...why don't you... ZZZZZZZZZZZZ."

Maya passed out, and when she awakened, her life would never be the same.

8

Saturday morning.

I was eating a bowl of cereal when I got a text from Ronald.

"Hey, Javon, are you watching the news?" Ronald asked excitedly!

"No, why?"

"Put on Channel 5 News, quick!"

"THIS IS NEWS CHANNEL 5! I'm Chuck Taylor. Today's top story! A tourist helicopter crashed into Littletown Tower. The 'copter is dangling on the media antenna on top of the building. From what we can see, it looks like the pilot and passengers are all okay, but who knows how long the helicopter will stay attached before it comes crashing down to the pavement? WHO WILL SAVE THEM?"

"You'll save them, Javon, right!?" asked Ronald sheepishly.

"I think so? I've never done anything like that before. Helicopters are huge, and it's really, really high!"

"SDK, you don't have a choice. You can't just let those people—"

"I know, I know," I yelled back. "OKAY! I'm on my way!"

———

I can't even remember the last time I put this suit on. Part of me is so excited to be the hero again! I just wonder if I'm in over my head.

I shimmied into the suit, which was getting a little tight. Gotta lay off the tacos.

Then I put on the mask and headed for the window. As I passed the mirror, I could see the look of fear on my face. *I'm just a kid*, I thought. Then I stood tall, took a deep breath...

"I GOT THIS!"

I opened the window and flew.

Jetting through the air is such an amazing feeling. As a little kid, I always dreamed of what it would feel like to soar among the clouds. When you're small you can feel powerless. Everything is bigger than you! Adults, trees, buildings, everything! But now as The Supadupa Kid, I feel strong, bold, unstoppable!

Just as I was thinking that, a pigeon flew right into my head.

"CRAW!" it yelped out.

"OW!" I screamed.

Maybe I should focus on flying and stop daydreaming before a plane hits me in the head!

The city was only a few miles away, and Littletown Tower was in the center. It's the tallest structure in the city by a lot, so it's easy to spot. As I got closer, I could see the helicopter's landing skids hooked onto the tower's antenna. Now, a hero like Superman or Wonder Woman could use their super strength to lift it up and float it gently to the ground. Well, I don't have super strength. The lightning strike that gave me the abilities to shoot lightning bolts and fly didn't grace me with extra strength. Sometimes I struggle opening a jar of peanut butter. When I do I hand it to Denise, and in no time,

POP! It's open! So if I can't open a jar of Skippy, how the heck am I going to lift a helicopter!?

As I flew closer, I noticed two things one good and one bad.

GOOD: The blades on the helicopter weren't moving.

BAD: The antenna wasn't very strong, and the wind was swaying the helicopter back and forth.

I could see that the passengers inside were all freaking out, and it wasn't just because they were trapped thousands of feet in the sky. They had just noticed that a kid in an orange superhero suit was floating in mid-air!

"Hey! It's okay! I'm here to help," I yelled.

They were perplexed, looking at me the way a dog looks at a vacuum cleaner, and we all know what happens when that vacuum cleaner is turned on...PANIC!

The sound of bending metal creaking took over the sound of my voice, and that's when the 'copter passengers really started to panic.

The antenna was bending, and the 'copter was leaning toward the side. The bend was slow but sure.

"AHHHHHHH!" The screams of the passengers and pilot were terrifying. *OH MY GOODNESS...*What am I going to do? I thought.

I don't have the strength to lift this thing. Maybe I could push it straight back up by flying. "IT'S GOING TO BE OKAY!" I yelled.

A little boy who couldn't have been more than six years old put his hand to the window. I could see the look of utter fear in his eyes. He mouthed the words, "Thank you."

I just nodded yes.

I can do this! I can do this...I think.

I went to the side of the 'copter that was bending and used my flying abilities to push it back to the upright antenna position. It seemed to be working. The antenna was bending back and the helicopter was back in its straight-up position. I guess I pushed a little too hard, and it bent in the opposite direction... and fast. So fast that the giant antenna snapped in half and the helicopter started plummeting to the ground!

I could hear the little boy scream, "MOMMY!"

NOOOOOOOOOOOOOO!

9

When Maya woke up, she couldn't believe the time.

The clock on her nightstand said 10:37am. *How in the world did I sleep that late? I never sleep past 8am on a Saturday,* Maya thought to herself. Maya went to the bathroom to brush her teeth.

As she looked into the mirror, she saw the amulet. It was so pretty. She had never seen such an amazing shade of red before. She would cherish it forever.

Just as she was putting toothpaste on her toothbrush, Marìa barged into the bathroom. "Sorry, Maya, I've got to get my hair brush. Mamà is taking me clothes shopping." Marìa bumped into Maya hard, eager to get her hair brush.

"MOVE!" Maya yelled.

Instantly Marìa was thrown out of the bathroom door as if someone lifted her up and tossed her on to the floor.

"OW, Maya, why did you push me so hard?"

"I barely touched you, Marìa. Are you okay?

"No, my booty hurts."

"I'm sorry, Marìa, I didn't...wait...I didn't do anything. How did that happen?" Shrugging, Maya handed Marìa her brush, gave her a hug, and kept brushing her teeth.

After getting dressed, Maya walked into the kitchen to find Mamà and Nana Hilda enjoying brunch.

"Good morning, sleepy head," Mamà said with a chuckle. "You sure slept late today."

"Yeah, I don't know why. I guess I was just tired."

"*Buenos días, Maya,*" said Nana Hilda.

"*Buenos días,* Nana. Thank you for the necklace, it's beautiful."

"That is very pretty, Maya, and what a nice gift, Nana."

"That necklace has been passed down for generations," said Nana proudly.

"How come you never gave it to me?" asked Mamà bitterly.

"You never needed it," Nana said as she winked at Maya.

A puzzled look came across Mamà's face. "Hmmm, okay!"

"Maya, I'm taking your sister and abuela out to shop for some clothes. You could use some yourself. Girls' day out!"

"Okay, Mamà. Let me get dressed," said Maya.

"Okay, but before you get dressed, can you please help me tidy up a little? I need you to clean the guest room for Nana, especially under the bed."

"Sure, Mamà, no problem. Marìa, wanna come and help me?"

"I'll be right there," said Marìa.

When Maya walked into the guest bedroom, she saw that it was a mess. The guest room had become a storage room. There were boxes of baby clothes, old toys and other things cluttering the room. She needed to put all of the boxes in the closet to make enough room for Nana to walk around without an avalanche of boxes hitting her on the head.

The very first box she grabbed said BOOKS. It was ridiculously heavy. She grunted as she tried to lift it. Panting and out of breath, she stood in front of the box with her hands on her hips. With clenched fists, she said, "I wish you would just MOVE yourself!" Maya felt a cold jolt on her neck, and simultaneously the box slid across the floor with the force of a speeding car. BOOM against the closed closet door.

She was stunned!

"GASP! WHAT!? HOW!? What just happened!?" she said out loud. She looked around the room, dumbfounded!

"How did that happen?" She grabbed the amulet. It was freezing cold a second ago, and now warm to the touch.

She went to the box and poked it, then kicked it. Maybe it was a ghost, but she didn't believe in ghosts.

She stepped back from the box, clenched her fists again and softly said, "MOVE." Slowly, the box came toward her like a crawling baby. Her eyes got really big, and her heart was pounding though her Beyoncé tee shirt. She didn't even notice that the amulet got cold again.

"STOP!" she yelled just as the box inched toward her slippers.

She put her hand over her mouth to stop herself from screaming.

Maya took a deep breath. She opened the closet door, looked at the box and said, "MOVE!"

Slowing, the box slid across the wooden floor, making a swooshing sound. Just as the box got into the back of the closet, she gently said "Stop." The box came to a halt, and Maya realized that she was clenching her hands so tightly that they were numb. She closed and locked the bedroom door so no one would come in.

She looked at the box marked baby clothes: "MOVE."

The box of linens: "MOVE."

The box of dishes, hats, electronics: "MOVE, MOVE, MOVE!"

In less than a minute, all the boxes were in the closet.

Next, under the bed... *Could I lift the bed?* Maya wondered.

"RISE!" she said, but the bed didn't move. She looked at the bed. Hmph!

"MOVE," she commanded as she raised her hands, palms up, and the bed slowly rose into the air!

Maya laughed in amazement. "How am I doing this?"

With the bed in the air, she looked across the room into the full-sized mirror and saw that the red amulet was glowing. A look of fear and shock came across her face. She stared in awe at the bed floating in the air, the bed that she had moved with just her thoughts and by uttering the word MOVE. That look of fear gradually turned into a smirk!

Suddenly there was a knock on the door.

"Maya, it's me. Why is the door locked?" Marìa asked.

Maya whispered "Move" and with a wave of her hands gently lowered the bed.

She looked in the mirror to see the glowing red amulet quickly dim, then opened the door.

"Hey, Marìa, I didn't need your help after all. I'm all done."

"How did you move all those heavy boxes by yourself?" Marìa asked skeptically.

"It's amazing what you can do when you put your mind to it!" Maya boasted.

10

"Mamà, can we go to the department store downtown? I love the clothes there," Marìa said excitedly.

"Of course, baby. I only plan on going into one store. Since Nana is with us, I don't want to do too much walking," Mamà said.

"YAY!" Marìa said joyfully.

"Maya, why are you so quiet?" Mamà asked.

Maya was still in shock from her newly discovered powers. As she sat in the back seat behind her Nana, she tried to understand what had just happened. All she knew was that the woman sitting right in front of her had given her these powers.

"Maya!"

"OH...yes, Mamà?"

"Why are you so quiet? Usually your mouth is going a mile a minute."

"Hmmm, I'm just excited to finally get some new clothes. Kinda speechless," she nervously chuckled.

"Oh Elizabeth, leave Maya alone. She's in her own new world," Nana said.

Maya wasn't used to hearing her mother called by her first name. And Nana was so right; this was a new world. Nana turned her head back to look at Maya. "A whole new world, right, Maya?" She smiled slyly and gave Maya a little wink.

Maya couldn't move; she couldn't even blink.

She shook herself and blurted out, "YES, a whole new world, a whole new world."

All of a sudden, they were at a standstill.

"Darn traffic. Looks like everyone is out shopping today," said Mamà.

They pulled up next to an older man changing a flat tire on the side of the road. Maya could see the man struggling to get the flat tire off of the car. His white shirt had streaks of black on it from trying to get the dirty tire off. Stomping his feet and grumbling, he marched to the trunk of his car to look for something to pry the tire off.

Maya whispered, "MOVE," and the flat tire spun off the car with ease, gently landing next to the spare that was lying on the ground. She then focused on the spare. "MOVE," she whispered again. The spare floated off the ground and locked in place where the flat was.

With a crow bar in hand, the gray haired man walked back to the wheel and couldn't believe what he saw. The flat tire was on the ground, and the spare was firmly in place.

"What in the world?" the man wondered, as he scratched his head in disbelief.

The man looked around to see who could have done this and locked eyes with Maya. Maya smiled, shrugged her shoulders, and looked away as traffic lightened up and they drove away.

A block away they found a parking space, and the four ladies started walking toward the department store. As they turned the corner, they could see there was a huge commotion. Hundreds of people were looking up at the sky. As Maya and her family looked up, they saw something huge dangling on top of a tall building.

They all heard a loud SNAP, and then the large object started falling to the ground. A second later, there was a loud KA-BOOM, and the Supadupa Kid appeared.

Maya gasped! She had heard about him but never seen him in person. All the girls in school talked about how cute and muscular he was. Maya thought he was kinda skinny.

"OH MY GOODNESS!" Mamà and Nana both yelled.

They could see that the object dropping from the sky was a helicopter. The crowd screamed, preparing for the crash. The Supadupa Kid was directly under the plummeting helicopter. He threw his hands in the air and formed a really cool-looking, crackling electric bubble. Maya could see the fear on his face and also that he looked familiar.

Nana looked at Maya and squeezed her hand as if to give her a signal to do something. *"¡Maya, ahora tienes el poder!"*

Yes, Nana, I have the power!

The 'copter was only a few yards away as it nose-dived directly at The Supadupa Kid at an incredible speed. As loudly as Maya could, she screamed, "MOVE!!!!"

11

SECONDS...

I only had seconds to save these people!

SECONDS...

With lightning speed I flew down to the sidewalk. Even I was shocked by how fast I flew down to the ground.

There was a crowd of bystanders who gasped in horror as the helicopter plummeted to the ground. Their screams were deafening.

The screaming stopped momentarily as I landed with a thunderous KA-BOOM on the sidewalk! I heard someone yell, "HEY, IT'S THE SUPADUPA KID!" I think that's when I was most terrified. I realized that it was up to me to save these people, and if I couldn't, it would somehow be my fault.

HOW AM I GOING TO DO THIS?

SECONDS...

I can't use my lightning bolts to slow them down because the electricity would toast them. Basically the helicopter is a metal box, and metal is a primary conductor of electricity. The people inside would be like toast in a toaster.

If I could somehow form a mild electrical force field, perhaps they would bounce off of it like a trampoline? They might get a few bumps and bruises but they would live, I hope.

SECONDS...

There was no time to think this through.

I have no idea if this will work!

I am so scared!

I looked up and saw the helicopter coming toward me with blazing speed. At first it looked like a small dot, and now it was a huge piece of machinery spinning violently.

I am so scared!

I quickly looked around to make sure no one was around me. Fortunately everyone was at a safe distance.

Not only could I hear the screams of the crowd, but also the screams of the passengers in the helicopter as it got closer.

I took a deep breath. SECONDS...

I threw my hands up in the air and formed a bubble of electricity. I had to make it hard enough that it would protect me from being crushed, but soft enough so that it would act like a giant electric rubber ball, allowing the aircraft to bounce off and land on the ground without too much force.

I screamed ...3, 2, 1... AHHHHHHHH!

12

The noise from the crowd drowned out Maya's yell. No one heard her scream except her Nana, who looked at her with such tremendous pride.

It was as if time stood still. The helicopter stopped immediately right above the electric bubble. IT. JUST. STOPPED. The crowd gasped.

The Supadupa Kid was looking up, face to face with the passengers from the helicopter. EVERYONE WAS SHOCKED!

———

I thought to myself, *WOW, IT WORKED*, I'm awesome! Then the helicopter started to glide to my left.

"Hey, I'm not doing this."

Without anyone noticing, Maya whispered "MOVE", waved her hands and swayed the helicopter so it was upright, then moved her hands to the left. The helicopter moved to the left and landed on the sidewalk with only a little THUD. The passengers opened the door and jumped out.

The crowd roared! THAT WAS AMAZING! WOW! INCREDIBLE!

The family and pilot hugged me as if I had just handed them a billion dollars. I have to admit: I felt so happy...and confused! *I didn't move the helicopter! I'm not even sure I stopped it from falling. What is going on here!?*

"SUPADUPA KID! SUPADUPA KID! SUPADUPA KID!" the crowd chanted. Firefighters, police officers, and EMT workers were now on the scene. It was crazy.

"Thank you, young man, for saving our lives," a woman from the helicopter said. "I knew you would save us," the little boy said, with tears in his eyes.

I just smiled and said, "You're welcome." Still bewildered! The crowd was cheering so loud, it was like a rock concert! There were hundreds of people, all screaming my name.

I waved to say thank you for their support, and immediately someone caught my eye. I know that girl. OMG! Could that be..."Maya?"

13

"The front page of the newspaper! Javon, you made the front page! You're a celebrity!" Ronald shouted.

While it felt awesome to be recognized in newspapers and on TV, I couldn't help but feel indifferent. *How did the helicopter stop? How did it float and land? I know I didn't do it. But who did and how did they do it?*

"Javon…are you listening?! You're on TV again! Man! You're a real-life star! Maybe we could start marketing your image on t-shirts and lunch boxes?"

"Yeah...lunch boxes," I said half-heartedly. "I mean, no! No lunch boxes or t-shirts. I've got to keep a low profile. The more we draw attention to The Supadupa Kid, the more likely we are to expose who's behind the mask! And I'm not ready for that kind of drama."

RING!

I was so startled by my cell phone ringing that I accidentally shot a lightning bolt near Ronald's feet. Fortunately we keep a fire extinguisher nearby, as this is a common occurrence.

"Hello! Hey, Javon, it's Maya. Did you forget about our date?"

"OH, SNAP! I'm on my way. Be there in 15 minutes. Bye!"

"Who was that?" asked Ronald.

"Maya."

"OH! señorita Cutie Pie!" Ronald said with a twinkle in his eye, while making a cat growl and clawing motion with his hands. "Prrrrrrr!"

"Dude! That's so creepy."

14

"I'm so sorry I was late, Maya. Things have been a little kooky lately." "Oh, really? How so?" asked Maya very suspiciously.

In my head I wanted to say, "Oh you know, cleaning up crime in the streets, saving citizens from peril...the usual."

"Just lots of homework," I said very awkwardly.

"Yeah, homework can be tough. Did you hear about the helicopter incident that happened yesterday?"

"Nope!" I said confidently, while in my head I was thinking, liar, liar, pants on fire.

"Really, Javon, it's all over the news. The Supadupa Kid saved an entire family. It was amazing! I was there. I saw the whole thing."

"I know...I MEAN...I know it must have been awesome to see that happen in person. I bet you think The Supadupa Kid is pretty cool, huh?"

"He's just okay."

"JUST OKAY?!" I screamed. "I mean... yeah...he's okay."

I gotta stop being so nervous.

"Haha! No. He's SUPA cool. The way he stopped that helicopter in mid air and saved that family was the most incredible thing I've ever seen. He's kinda cute, too." Maya chuckled.

That's more like it, I thought to myself.

"Say, you wanna get an ice cream? I think I see a stand over there."

"Sure!" Maya said happily.

"Excuse me, Mr. Ice Cream Man. Can I get a large vanilla cone with chocolate sprinkles? Maya, what would you like?"

"I'll have the same," she said softly with glee.

The vendor handed me my cone. Then he attempted to give Maya hers, but he accidentally dropped it.

"Oops!" he yelled.

As it was falling to the ground, I thought I heard Maya say something. Suddenly the cone seemed to slow down. Like the wind caught it and stopped it from falling.

Maya quickly scooped her hand under the cone. "GOT IT!" Maya yelped happily as she started licking her ice cream. The ice cream man and I just looked at each other. Did we both see what we thought we saw?

"Come on, Javon, let's keep walking."

I must have been seeing things, right?

15

Ms. Burnett is one of my favorite teachers. She makes social studies fun. Today was the big book report day. All the students had to write a report about the place they're most interested in outside of the United States, and tell the class about it. My report was about China. China has such great history and culture. Not to mention, their food is the bomb!

The Treacherous Three convinced Ms. Burnett to let them do their report together. *This should be a train wreck!* "Okay. The Thomas girls are up next, and then you, Maya. Let's go, ladies," said Ms. Burnett.

Tracy, Tanya and Tammy got up together and walked toward the front of the classroom, strutting in unison as if they had rehearsed it. Then they turned to face the class, snapped their fingers and even started to recite their book report in unison. The only thing more annoying than the Thomas Triplets is the Thomas Triplets reading together.

All I could hear for 10 minutes was "BLAH, BLAH, BLAH...BLAH, BLAH, BLAH, BLAH, BLAH, and that's why we love Paris!"

After they were done, they snapped their fingers, sashayed back to their seats and glided into their chairs, all in unison. UGH!

"Thank you, ladies. According to your report, Paris is nothing but expensive shoes, clothes, and food," Ms. Burnett said sarcastically, as all the students snickered.

"Okay, Maya, you're up!"

With her report in hand, Maya walked to the front of the class. As soon as she got there, she slipped and fell.

"Owwwww!"

The class busted out laughing, but it wasn't funny. You could see she really hurt herself. As Ms. Burnett helped her up, she saw a wet spot in the floor. She bent down and rubbed her fingers on the wet spot and realized it was soap. She stood up with her hands on her hips and sternly said, "Ladies, did you spill this on the floor?"

"I don't know what you're talking about, Ms. Burnett," they said together.

"Javon, please help Maya to the nurse's office. Ladies, you three are to stay after class so we can straighten this out!"

Maya put her arm around my shoulder as I assisted her down the hall. I hated that she was hurt, but I have to admit, I kinda liked her leaning on me.

As we walked out of the classroom, I heard Maya whisper something. It sounded like the word she said when she caught her ice cream cone. It sounded like she said the word, "move." Then I heard WAP! WAP! WAP! The Treacherous Three got slapped in the face with their notebooks. "OW!" they each screamed, holding their noses like they just got punched.

"That'll show 'em," Maya sneered.

Just then I saw a look in her eyes that really worried me. Maya was really angry. The Thomases were pushing her to the limit. As tough as Maya is, I know she's not crazy enough to take on three girls, especially those three nuts!

Out of the corner of my eye, I saw a flash of red light around Maya's neck....or maybe I was just seeing things...again.

16

A few days had passed since Maya almost broke her butt bone, and despite how angry she was at first, she seemed really happy now. The Treacherous Three got suspended for a day and had to write an apology to Maya, but the letter wasn't sincere at all.

> Dear Maya,
>
> We are so sorry you fell. Be more careful next time.
>
> T, T, T.

I had a feeling that Maya was just waiting for the perfect time to get them back. She's too tough to just let that slide.

Anyway, today is a big day. We have a class trip to the Museum of Natural History. I love that place. There's so much to learn and see. We all got paired up, and I got to hang with Maya, which made me supadupa happy. Ronald got paired up with Tracy. I'm not sure who I felt more sorry for! Ronald is going to talk her head off, and Tracy may turn Ronald into stone with her Medusa glare.

We walked through the space exploration area, dinosaur age area, and so many more. For lunch we had to brown bag it. My mom made tuna. YUCK! Come on, Mom! You know I'm a PB&J kinda dude.

The museum had closed off the section that featured a Mexican exhibit just for our school. Maya was thrilled because of her Mexican heritage. She told me stories that her Nana told her about the Maya Civilization that she was named after.

"The Maya are a very proud and strong people. They were known for their amazing architecture, science, astrology and mathematics," Maya boasted.

"Did somebody say science?" Ronald yelped with enthusiasm.

"No, Ronald, go back to boring Tracy," I said.

"OH, OKAY!" Ronald said without missing a beat.

"What were you saying, Maya?"

"I was saying that the Maya were really evolved. Their civilization was very sophisticated and complex. Look at this, Javon."

Maya read from the plaque next to an ancient mask.

"This mask was used by Maya warriors to fight in war by harnessing the powers of the cosmos. It says here that anyone who wears the mask will absorb the stars' energy and can become invisible to their enemies in time of battle."

"WHOA! That sounds dope! A little too superhero-like for me," I said with a smirk, "but I can't imagine how cool it would be to be invisible."

Tracy heard everything Maya said. She pulled her sisters together and said,

"I want that mask! I'm going to make a distraction, and I want you to grab it, okay, Tammy?"

"Duh, I don't think that's a good idea, Tracy. We could get in a lot of trouble," Tammy said in a sheepish tone.

"Hey! I'm the oldest, and you have to do what I say!"

"Duh...you're the oldest by only four minutes," Tanya scoffed.

"Just grab it when the alarm goes off!" Tracy demanded.

"ALARM?!" Tammy and Tanya said as they gasped.

"Ms. Burnett, may I go to the bathroom?" Tracy asked, looking coy.

"Okay, but come right back. We're about to continue with the tour."

"Sure thing, Ms. Burnett!"

Tracy scooted out of the area looking for the fire alarm. She didn't have to go far before she found it. She looked around to make sure no one was watching, and then...

RING!!!!!

It was pandemonium!

The sound was so loud, I couldn't think. What could have caused the alarm?! I looked for smoke or some emergency, but there was nothing out of the ordinary.

Ms. Burnett gathered us all together and rushed us out of the area.

Tammy and Tanya did as they were told. They took the mask off the display and put it in the backpack. Tracy caught up with the rest of us as we plowed out of the museum and back on to the school bus.

"Hey, Ronald," I said as we were heading back to school. "Too bad the day was cut short. You didn't even get to see the Thomas Edison exhibit."

"Snif...I know," said Ronald.

The bus ride was silent except for an occasional snicker from T3 sitting in the back seat.

17

The next morning, school was back to normal...kinda.

Ronald was super sad that we had to cut the museum trip short. He was moping around like someone stole his microscope. Maya was more quiet than usual. She looked so focused. Like she knew a storm was coming.

But what was really unusual was the silence coming from the Treacherous Three. Any other time you can't shut them up! Today, not a peep.

During lunch I sat with Ronald and Maya. We were yapping about nothing in particular.

The T3 were sitting behind us. I turned around occasionally because they were strangely quiet. They all had weird looks on their faces. I could see Tanya to my left, Tammy to my right, and Tracy in the middle.

I turned back to talk to Ronald, then I heard a gasp from the triplets. When I looked back at them, Tracy was gone. How did she disappear so fast? I looked around the cafeteria and didn't see her. Why did it look like Tammy and Tanya had seen a ghost?

"Javon!"

"Yeah...oh, hey, Maya."

"Is there something wrong?" questioned Maya.

As I turned back around, I saw that Tracy was back in her seat. Puzzled, I said, "No, everything is cool."

But I was thinking that something strange was going on.

When school was over, Maya and Marìa took their usual path home through the Bald Spot. The two of them were holding hands. Maya walked at a steady pace, while Marìa skipped and sang "LA, LA, LA," swinging Maya's arms happily. Out of nowhere, their arms were forcibly separated, like someone yanked them apart.

"Ouch," Marìa said.

Then Maya was pushed to the ground, and her books flew across the dirt.

"Why did you fall down?" Marìa asked, confused.

"I didn't fall. I was pushed," Maya said sternly. She thought she heard a low, sinister giggle. Maya got up and was immediately pushed down again.

"Why do you keep falling down?" cried Maria.

"I'm not!!!! Something is pushing me."

"I'm scared, Maya."

"Don't be!" One of Maya's books flew from the dirt and hit her in the head. WHACK!

"OUCH!"

"Maya! The wind is throwing books at you!" Maria cried.

"I don't think this is the wind," Maya said, as another book propelled from the ground toward her head.

"MOVE!" Maya yelled, throwing her hands toward the flying book. The book stopped and boomeranged until she heard a THUD! The book appeared to stop in mid-air and then fell to the ground. Both Maya and Maria heard someone yell "OW," then they saw footprints in the dirt running away.

The two sisters just looked at each other.

"Maya?"

"Yes, Maria?"

"Are you a witch?"

18

When they got home, Maya looked in the bathroom mirror and saw the newest bump on her forehead from the flying book.

"I must have the bumpiest head in the city."

She was bewildered. *How did that book fly from the ground directly at me? And what about those footprints running away? And I know I heard someone say OW.*

Maria knocked on the door.

"Maya, can I come in?"

"Sure."

"Maya, I'm scared. I don't want to walk home after school anymore. And how did you stop that book from hitting you? I saw you stop it. How did you do that?"

Maya gave a big sigh.

"Marìa, you're my little sister. I love you more than anything in the world, and with love comes trust. Can I trust you?"

"*Sí*, Maya, you can trust me."

"Okay, I'm going to show you something, but it has to be a secret. Can you keep a secret? You can't tell anyone, and I mean anyone!"

"I can, cross my heart," Marìa said seriously.

"Okay..."

Maya took a deep breath and opened her arms wide. Looking at Marìa with an expression that showed just how much she loved and trusted her sister, Maya whispered, "MOVE."

Slowly, Marìa floated upward and toward Maya. She immediately gasped out of fear until the butterflies in her tummy made her giggle.

"Maya, how are you doing this?" Marìa asked, as she gently floated into Maya's waiting arms. Maya gave her the biggest hug, kissed her on her nose and with a tear falling down her cheek said, "I don't know." As the glowing red amulet shone between them both.

19

Tammy said to Tracy, "I don't think this is a good idea. Mom and Dad would kill us if we were caught shoplifting."

"We're not going to get caught. We can't get caught because I can't be seen, and whatever I touch can't be seen either. Plus, don't you love this outfit? I think I'm going to wear it to the big dance with these killer shoes! They are so hot! I'm going into the dressing room, and when I come out, I'll be the cutest looking girl in the mall."

"Duh...except no one will be able to see you, Tracy," Tanya said scratching her head.

"Whatever, Tanya," Tracy said as she rolled her eyes. "Give me the backpack, Tammy."

Tammy reluctantly handed the back-pack over. Tanya and Tammy stood there, helplessly watching Tracy walk into the dressing room. They both knew this was wrong, but just like when they were little kids, Tracy was always the one in charge. This moment felt like the time in the first grade when Tanya found their teacher's wallet on the side of her desk. It was just as class ended and they were leaving for the day. Tammy picked it up and started to hand it to Ms. Brown, who was speaking to Billy López about his constant nose-picking and smearing his boogers on the back of everyone's shirt. So gross! Because of that he got the nickname Billy-Booger-Back, which has stuck to this day.

Anyway, just before Tammy went to tug on Ms. Brown's dress to give her wallet back, Tracy grabbed Tammy's hand and took the wallet away from her. She put it in her Princess Buttercup lunchbox and never gave it back. Tammy and Tanya stood there helplessly, knowing that Tracy could do whatever she wanted, whenever she wanted. It was just her way.

Now, Tammy and Tanya stood just as helplessly in the clothing store outside the dressing room. They could only see Tammy's feet under the door. She put on the outfit and the new shoes. Then in a flash, her feet disappeared. The door creaked open, and Tammy and Tanya could see the impressions of footsteps on the plush store carpet.

Tracy sternly whispered, "Let's go." Passing the clerk behind the dressing room counter, who didn't notice a thing.

Tanya and Tammy walked swiftly toward the exit. Tracy was behind them... at least, they thought she was behind them. As they approached the exit, the security guard greeted them with a tip of his hat and said, "Have a nice day, ladies."

"You too, sir," Tanya and Tammy said together. As the automatic door swung open, the alarm went off.

"Excuse me, ladies. Do you mind coming back here?"

Tammy and Tanya said frightfully, "No, sir. We don't mind." They looked at each other in fear.

"I'll meet you outside," Tracy whispered just loud enough for the security guard to hear.

"You'll meet me where?" asked the guard.

"We didn't say anything, sir," Tanya said.

"Nope, not a thing, sir," Tammy said.

"Hmph. I thought I heard one of you ladies say something. This darn hearing aid is on the fritz again." The guard pulled out an alarm detector that looked like a long paddle and waved it up and down over the girls. It didn't make a sound.

With a puzzled look on his face, he said, "Well...I guess this alarm system works as well as my hearing aid. You ladies can go. Have a nice day, now!"

"You too, sir," the girls said with a sigh of relief. After walking a couple of yards, they were startled by a loud **"BOO!"**

"AHHHHHH!" they both screamed!

"HAHA! You two suckers almost got arrested."

"That wasn't funny, Tracy. We could

have gotten in big trouble," Tanya said, turning around. She saw nothing but could smell the scent of Tracy's designer perfume.

"Oh, please!" Tracy said sarcastically. "Here! Take the mask and put it in the backpack. I want to make sure it doesn't get damaged. I need it to teach Maya a lesson tomorrow at the big dance."

Poof!

Just like that Tracy appeared in her new cute outfit. Her hair and makeup were absolutely perfect. So was the sneer on her face.

Tanya put the mask in the backpack, and the girls hopped into the back of their dad's limo and drove off.

What the girls didn't see was that Ronald and his parents were in the mall too, and he saw everything. EVERYTHING!

20

"Hey, Denise, can you please pass the asparagus?" I asked.

"Gladly! You know I don't like these green sticks of death! BLAH!"

"You're going to eat at least a few sticks of death, Denise," Dad stated.

"John!" Mom yelled. "We don't call our food death sticks!"

"Technically I said 'sticks of death,' not 'death sticks'...there's a difference," Denise said with a chuckle.

RING!!!!!!

"Javon, you know you're not supposed to bring your phone to the table!" Mom scolded.

"Oops! Sorry, Mom. I thought I had it on silent. It's Ronald. Can I answer it?"

"Boy! If you don't put that phone down at this table!" Mom said with a look that made my head hurt. Last time she looked at me like that, I had to wash all the Thanksgiving Day dinner dishes by myself, by hand, in the dark! Okay, I wasn't in the dark, but it was hard.

I pressed cancel and went back to eating. Immediately the phone rang again. UGH! I forgot to put it on silent.

"Give me the phone, Javon, NOW!" Mom demanded. I pressed cancel and handed it to Denise to pass it to Mom. Denise looked like she just won a year's supply of candy with that crooked smile on her face! Whenever I get in trouble, which has been a lot lately, Denise jumps for joy because not only do I get in trouble, but my punishment usually involves me doing one of her chores! Looks like I'm cleaning hamster poop for a month.

"Javon! You're cleaning the hamster cage for the rest of the month!"

"I saw that coming!" I said under my breath. *What could be so important that Ronald would keep calling?*

After dinner I did a little begging and pleading to Mom to get my phone back. The puppy dog eyes usually work, but not this time. So I had to barter. I told her not only would I clean the hamster poop, but I'd also wash the dishes, which was usually Dad's job. I said it really loudly so Dad would hear me.

"Give him back his phone, Honey," Dad said with a hint of glee.

"Okay, I'll give it back, but only because your grades have been stellar."

I could see Dad grinning from ear to ear as he gave himself a high-five! My dad is such a dork. Love that dude!

"Thanks, Mom," I said. I gave her a kiss on the cheek and snatched it out of her hands. "Oh, no he didn't," she said as I ran into my room and closed the door.

Not only had Ronald called me several times, but he texted me about a gazillion times to call him back. I called him immediately, and the phone rang for .01 seconds before he picked it up, screaming!

"JAVON, you're not going to believe what I just saw!!!!"

21

Late that night in the house of the Thomases, Tracy couldn't sleep. She was so excited about the mask and its ability to make her invisible, but she also remembered that there was another power. The power of the cosmos. *What does that even mean?!*

"Hey Siri, search the web for 'What is the cosmos?'

"Here's what I found," Siri said in her robotic voice:

Many astronomers believe that almost all of the cosmos was made of regular matter (protons, neutrons and electrons). However, they have now discovered that regular matter makes up only a small fraction. Astronomers have been able to determine that there is also invisible matter. They know that because even though they cannot see it, they are able to measure the effects of gravity on stars and planets. This invisible matter is what we call "dark matter".

There is also something that makes up most of the Universe and that we refer to as "dark energy". The nature of this dark energy is completely unknown, but we know it behaves quite differently from regular matter. It is believed that it has the opposite effect of gravity, which pushes everything apart, and thus contributes to the expansion of the Universe.

"Gravity! Can this mask control gravity?" Tracy reached underneath her bed and grabbed the backpack containing the mask. Her hands trembled with excitement, and she placed the mask on her face. She held her hand in front of her and saw it disappear instantly. Then she concentrated on the bed she was on. It only took a single thought, and with the greatest of ease, the bed floated up toward the ceiling. Stunned by how quickly the bed rose, she hit her head on the ceiling. THUMP! "Ow," she cried, rubbing her head. She thought the bed back down, and it glided to the floor. She took off the mask.

"DARK MATTER," she said with an evil grin. "I am DARK MATTER."

22

The whole school was abuzz because of the big dance that night. It was the first big dance of the school year, and you could tell. Everyone was talking about what they were going to wear, who they were going to dance with, and most importantly, who the DJ was. It was none other than local legend, DJ Ace In The Hole, or just DJ ACE. He's a big deal around here because not only did he graduate from our school, but he also tours with some of the biggest pop stars in the world. He's also Principal Johnson's cousin, which is dope.

I was excited about the dance also, but after what Ronald had told me, I had other things to be concerned about. As we sat in Ms. Burnett's class, I could see the backpack Ronald had mentioned. Tracy had it slung around her shoulder and looked like she had no desire to take it off. I had to see if the mask was in there.

When class ended, I followed her to our next class, which was in the library. I looked for an opportunity to grab it and run, but Tanya and Tammy were vigilant. They saw me staring at the backpack and whispered something into Tracy's ear. Tracy stopped, turned around, and looked at me dead in the eye. I have to admit I was kinda scared of her. She's like the cute version of the Wicked Witch of the West in The Wizard of Oz, minus the broom.

What do you want, Javon!?" she shouted as she poked her finger into my chest, which really hurt. I've got to be the world's weakest superhero. Batman would be so disappointed.

"Ummm, nothing, Tracy. I was just admiring your, er...hair! It looks so shiny." *Nice one, Javon. That was pretty much the dumbest thing I've ever said.*

"Loser!" she said as her sisters repeated, "LOSER!" Tracy snapped her fingers and said, "Girls, bathroom, now!"

"Yes, Tracy," Tanya and Tammy said obediently.

As they strutted into the bathroom, Ronald and I looked at each other.

"Now what?" Ronald asked.

"I don't know. Let's head to the library."

Library class was time to catch up on school work, study, read, or do homework. A lot of kids just messed around or took a nap. I usually used it as time to read or talk to BrainBoy about Supadupa stuff. Maya sat with us, so that wasn't happening today.

We sat down, then Tanya and Tammy

walked in with no sign of Tracy. Ronald and I looked at each other.

"OH, BOY!" Ronald mumbled. "I don't like the feeling of this." "What's going on?" Maya asked.

All of a sudden there was a piercing scream. It sounded just like Tracy, except she was nowhere to be found. Then books just started flying off of the shelves. Thousands of them. They flew around the room like missiles, knocking down students and causing havoc. Ronald, Maya and I, along with all the students in the library, hid under the table to protect ourselves. Mr. Dews, the librarian, screamed, "OH MY WORD! OH MY WORD!"

"What are you going to do, Javon?" Ronald shouted over the sound of pages fluttering in the air. Maya looked at both Ronald and me, confused.

"What is he supposed to do?" Maya yelled. Books were slamming against the wall, through the windows, and striking the floor, ceiling, and table tops. Maya got the strangest look on her face and took a deep breath.

"This isn't the first time I've dealt with flying books!" Maya exclaimed. "BOYS... BRACE YOURSELVES!" She threw out her hands and yelled, "MOVE!"

All the books that were flying fast and furiously stopped in mid-air and fell to the floor. THUD, THUD, THUD, THUD, THUD, THUD, THUD.

"WOW!" both Ronald and I said to each other. Then we looked at Maya. We both noticed a red glow coming from under her t-shirt. She clutched it, looked at us and said, "I can explain."

23

After the school nurse gave Mr. Dews some smelling salts to wake him up from his fainting spell, all of the students helped pick up the books and put them back on the shelves.

When school was over, Maya and I went to Ronald's house, where she told us about the amulet her grandmother had given her. I was honored that she trusted us with such a secret.

"Who else knows about this?" Ronald asked.

"Just my Nana and my little sister, Marìa, and now you two. I feel like I can trust you."

Ronald and I looked at each other with the exact same thought. "Should we tell her?" we both asked at the same time.

Then it hit me!

"WAIT A MINUTE! YOU'RE THE ONE WHO STOPPED THE HELICOPTER!" I yelled.

And then it hit Maya. "WAIT A MINUTE! YOU'RE THE SUPADUPA KID!"

"OH MY GOSH!" we screamed.

"WAIT A MINUTE, I'M THE ONLY ONE HERE WITHOUT SUPERPOWERS!" Ronald cried.

"Okay! I know we are having a moment here, but we have a serious problem. Tracy has superpowers too, and she's pretty tough. How are we going to stop her?" Ronald asked.

"Together!" I said boldly. I stuck my hand out, and Ronald slapped his hand on top of mine. We both looked at Maya and nodded for her to join us. She smiled the most beautiful smile and slapped her hand on top of mine and Ronald's. Unfortunately she slapped it a little too hard, and a lightning bolt shot out of my fingertips and started a small fire on Ronald's carpet.

"In the name of Nikola Tesla, you've got to be more careful, Javon. That's the fourth carpet you've toasted this year. Maya, please hand me the fire extinguisher behind you, thanks."

After Ronald put out the fire, he said, "Maya, you're about the same height as Javon, right?"

"Yeah, why?"

"Cool." BrainBoy's eyes lit up and he rubbed his hands together and snickered devilishly. He ran to his closet and pulled out a box marked "DO NOT TOUCH."

"When I ordered Javon's Supadupa suit, I messed up and ordered the wrong color. I decided to keep it just in case he needed a backup. Turns out it would be better suited for his partner. YOU!"

The suit was shiny black and super cool. She went into the bathroom and tried it on.

"It's tight," she squawked.

"Have you ever seen a frumpy superhero outfit? I think not!" Ronald said smugly. Maya walked out looking like the coolest hero of all time.

"How does it look?" she asked.

Ronald and I just stood there with our mouths wide open. I may have drooled a little.

"BOYS!"

"YEAH! OH! WOW! You look, hmmm, nice! Right, Ronald? RIGHT, RONALD?!" I asked while slapping him in the back of his head.

"Ow, oh, yeah, you look, ahem, nice."

I went to the bathroom and put on my Supadupa suit and mask, which I keep in my back pack. When I walked out, Maya was looking at herself in the mirror. I stood next to her. Ronald handed her a mask. She gave me a sly look and put it on. We smiled.

"Let's party," she said.

24

Maya, Ronald and I entered the gymnasium and were completely wowed! The school really outdid itself for this party. There were disco glitter balls, strobe lights, streamers, balloons and everything you could imagine for a really cool party! DJ Ace In The Hole was pumping, playing that new hit song, 'TURN IT UP'! He was on stage with his DJ equipment, two of the largest speakers I've ever seen on each side of him, and above him were the letters A.C.E. It was by far the coolest party I've ever been to...which isn't saying a lot considering that I've never been to a party that didn't involve cake, ice cream and a really creepy clown.

It seemed like every student and teacher in the school was there, dancing like they had all just won the lottery. Even the custodian, old Mr. Bookman, was dancing...except he was dancing with a mop. Poor Mr. Bookman hasn't been the same since that bucket fell on his head.

I was scanning the room looking for The Treacherous Three when Maya nudged me and pointed to the far side of the gym. There they were, all three of them. Tracy was wearing an outfit that was different than Tammy and Tanya, which was out of the ordinary. And Tracy was wearing her backpack. The three of us nodded and walked toward them. As we walked through the dancing crowd, we lost sight of them. By the time we got to the corner of the gym, Tracy was gone.

"Hey, Tammy, where's Tracy?" Maya yelled over the music.

"She could be anywhere," Tammy said with an evil grin.

"Yeah, anywhere," Tanya said with the same tone. Then I heard in my right ear Tracy whisper, "Yeah, anywhere." I was startled to turn around and see that she wasn't there. Then in my other ear I heard Tracy again...

"I'm right here. Wanna go for a ride?"

"GASP!"

All of a sudden I was lifted up propelled toward a cement wall. Just as I was bracing myself to smash into it, I heard Maya yell, "MOVE." A nearby cluster of balloons jumped in front of me, cushioning me from being splattered. POP, POP, POP!

Maya was picked up into the air and started flying toward me. I grabbed her just before she hit the wall, and we both landed on the floor, face to face. For a fraction of a second, our noses and lips were right next to each other. That second seemed like an hour as I was so close to kissing her.

I could see something big coming toward us fast. It was Ronald. Maya stuck out her hand and yelled, "MOVE!" Ronald stopped in mid-air and plopped right on top of us.

"You've got to lighten up on the cupcakes, BrainBoy," I grunted as he tried to shimmy off of us.

You would think that the crowd would see what was going on and freak out, but the music was so loud, and everyone was having such a great time, no one noticed.

"How are we going to stop her if we can't see her?" Maya asked.

"I have an idea. Follow me," Ronald exclaimed.

25

The official colors of Booker T. Washington Middle School are red and gold. Those colors are everywhere. Teachers and students are always rocking red and gold t-shirts. Our mascot, Booker T. Eagle, has feathers that are red and gold. Our gym floor, our flagpole, and our freshly painted walls are also red and gold. During the last summer break, Principal Johnson recruited about 100 students, including Ronald and me, to paint the hallways. It was hard work but a lot of fun.

The students of Booker T. Washington, also known as the Bookers, are very proud of our school, and we express it in our school spirit. Everyone who participated in painting the halls still feels an even greater sense of pride when we walk down the hallways and see the results of our hard work. The one hallway everyone hates however is the hallway that leads to the maintenance room. That's where Mr. Bookman keeps all of his tools, brooms, mops, and the buckets of red and gold paint. We had to walk up and down those stairs a gazillion times carrying those heavy buckets of paint. Also down that hallway are the boiler room, air conditioning room, and water supply room. And that's exactly where Ronald was taking us.

"Ronald! What are we doing down here?" I asked.

"You'll see!" We reached the maintenance room. Ronald turned the doorknob. It was locked.

"Jeepers, it's locked."

"Jeepers," Maya repeated with a smirk.

"You'll get used to it," I said with a shrug.

"Hey, Javon, can you zap the door down?" As soon as Ronald made the request, Maya casually said, "MOVE," and the door fell like a chopped-down tree.

"Thanks!" Ronald said gratefully.

In the back of the room there were about a dozen cans of red and gold paint.

"Okay, each of you take two buckets of red paint and follow me," Ronald said confidently .

"Is he always this bossy?" Maya asked me.

"Usually only during science fair week," I said.

We grabbed all the paint we could carry and went across the hall to the water supply room, which was also locked.

"Maya, if you would be so kind," Ronald said very gentlemanlike.

"MOVE," Maya said, while flicking her finger as if she was flinging at a gnat. The door fell, and we went inside. There were a bunch of pipes, drains and other industrial things.

"Now, each of you open a jar of paint and pour it into the drain that says 'main water supply'."

"WHY?!" I yelled.

"Just do it!" Ronald yelled back.

When BrainBoy speaks, I listen. We poured the red paint into the drain and ran back to the party.

The party and music were still going strong. It looked like everyone was having a really good time, including Mr. Sykes, who was now dancing with Ms. Burnett.

"Get your groove on, Mr. Sykes," Ronald yelled.

We looked over the crowd for T3 and found two of them in front of DJ ACE's stage. Of course, we couldn't see Tracy, but I knew she was there.

Then the speakers that were on the far corners of the stage started floating and banging up and down really hard.

BOOM! BOOM! BOOM!

Everyone thought it was part of the show, but from the surprised look in DJ ACE's face, I knew it wasn't. It was Tracy!

"How is Tracy doing this?" Maya shouted.

"I don't know," I said, "but we've got to find out and stop her before she hurts someone."

"Well, to stop her, first we have to see her. It's time for The Supadupa Kid and Maya to crash the party," Ronald said.

"Call me *Muévete!*" Maya yelled.

"WHAT?"

"Muévete! (Mu Wev Ah Tay) It's Spanish! It means 'MOVE IT'," Maya said proudly.

"That's dope!" I said.

"I concur, " Ronald proclaimed.

I clapped my hands together and created a flash of light that blocked the crowd from seeing me undress and seeing my Supadupa suit. Maya had just taken off her jacket, put on her mask, and was ready to rumble.

When the flash disappeared, The Supadupa Kid and Muévete stood proud. The crowd caught sight of us and started clapping. Then the music stopped, and DJ ACE yelled into the microphone: "THE SUPADUPA KID IS IN THE HOUSE!!!!!!!!!!"

Everybody cheered.

"Make it rain, SDK!" Ronald said, while pointing to the ceiling and the sprinkler system.

"Ahhhh! I see now, BrainBoy," I said, as I patted him on his back, and accidentally gave him a little shock.

"OUCH!" Ronald yelped.

"My bad, Bro."

"You two got it from here. I'll lead the crowd out to safety."

I looked at Maya, so proud to have her by my side. I rubbed my hands together and made a crackling ball of electricity. I threw it toward the ceiling. It created what looked like a fireworks burst. The fire sprinkler system kicked in, and water started falling from the ceiling. At first the crowd thought it was cool, until the water started turning red and everyone ran, screaming, out of the gym. Ronald held the doors open, leading everyone to safety.

The water was cascading down, turning everything red. In the middle of the gym stood a red figure. The more paint fell on her, the more it looked like Tracy. Her fists were clenched, her clothes and hair were dripping red, and she was wearing something on her face. It was a mask. I quickly recognized that it was the mask from the museum!

"Ahhhhhh!" the figure yelled, as she waved her hands toward DJ ACE's giant speakers. They both floated off the stage and were hurled in our direction. One speaker flew toward me and the other toward Muévete.

I shot a lightning bolt at one speaker, shattering it into a thousand pieces.

"MOVE!" Muévete yelled, and the other speaker, which had to weigh about a ton, stopped mid-air and was hurled back at the figure. With a wave of her hand, the figure flung it against the wall effortlessly.

The red water was still falling and covering all of us. We stood before the figure, and I asked, "Tracy, is that you?"

"I am no longer Tracy. I am Dark Matter! Feel my wrath!" She now waved her hands at the large A.C.E. letters that hung above the DJ booth. They detached from the chains that held them up and flew at us. Then she waved her hands towards the bleachers. They broke off from the side of the gym and were sent hurtling toward us.

Muévete yelled, "MOVE," at the flying letters, deflecting them away from us. I shot a lightning bolt at the wooden bleachers that were about to crush us, blasting them into smithereens.

When the debris from the explosion disappeared, Dark Matter was gone, but we could see red footprints exiting the building. I started to fly after her when Muévete pointed to the sign that said "POOL", then pointed to us, soaking wet and covered in red paint.

"GOOD IDEA," I exclaimed.

After a quick dip in the pool to rinse the red paint off of us, we followed the red paint tracks to the football field. Dark Matter was standing perfectly still in the middle of the field. We approached her carefully. It was eerie.

"Tracy, I don't know how you are doing this, but this madness has to stop before someone gets hurt," I yelled out.

"Yeah! We all know you're a jerk and a meany but this is supremely crazy," Muévete shouted.

"You're not helping," I told Muévete.

"Oh, sorry. I'm new at this superhero thingy. Is there a superhero manual I can brush up on?"

"SILENCE! Tracy is gone. Only Dark Matter resides in this body. The mask says so!"

"The mask! We've got to get that mask off of her," I told Muévete.

"Behold the power of Dark Matter," she said with an evil tone.

She raised her arms, and the turf on the field began to tremble. Massive amounts of dirt shot up and consumed me and Muévete. We were coughing and gagging while being suffocated by the dirt. I spun around at supadupa speed, like a whirlwind, to funnel the dirt away from us.

Muévete yelled, "MOVE," and the dirt was propelled toward Dark Matter. With a wave from her hand, the dirt parted around her as she chuckled.

"You two are no match for Dark Matter." She reached out her arms toward the goal posts at the opposite ends of the football field. The posts came out of the dirt and launched at us. As Muévete opened her mouth, Dark Matter snapped her fingers, and a glob of dirt filled her mouth. Because Muévete wasn't able to speak and stop the posts, they slammed down upon us and forked us into the ground.

Without super strength, I couldn't push the goal posts off of me, and Muévete was struggling to get the dirt out of her mouth to move them. When she finally did, Dark Matter hurled two cars at us! My hands were pinned down to the ground and I couldn't get a good shot to destroy the cars that were about to crush us.

Muévete managed to spit out the dirt and yell as loudly as she could, "MOVE!!" The cars stopped just as they were a few feet away from crushing us. She yelled, "MOVE," again, sending the cars and goal posts in the direction of Dark Matter. She waved her hands, and the cars flew behind her, but the posts landed into the ground, standing straight up like two tuning forks on either side of her.

"HA! You missed," gloated Dark Matter.

"No, I didn't!" Focused on the goal posts, Muévete yelled, "MOVE!"

The goal posts started vibrating, lightly at first, then gradually louder and stronger. The sound was deafening. Dark Matter started to shake and shiver uncontrollably as she stood between the two pulsating posts. They were vibrating at such a high frequency that the school windows started to burst. Dark Matter was holding her ears, trying to block out the sound, but it was too strong. She fell to her knees as Muévete's nose started to bleed from the power coming from her. Then she yelled to me, "SUPADUPA, light it up!"

"My pleasure! KABOOM SUCKA!"

I shot a lightning bolt at each of the posts, sending shockwaves between them. The vibration of the goal posts, along with the energy from my blast, brought Dark Matter down to the ground. Her mask shook off and fell, shattering it into fragments.

Muévete waved her hands, and the vibrations stopped. When we walked toward Tracy, she was lying on the ground in a fetal position. Muévete grabbed one arm, and I grabbed the other as we helped her up. When she got to her feet, she asked dazed and confused. "Where am I?"

"You're at the football field," I told her.

"Was there a game? Who won?"

"We did. Two to nothing," Muévete said with a smirk.

"Why am I covered in red? It's not really my color," Tracy said, confused.

"You're the mascot," I told her.

We helped her up and walked her to the sidelines. Sirens were wailing in the background, which was our cue to get outta there.

"Tracy, you're going to be okay. Police and EMT's are on their way." Tammy and Tanya, who looked shaken, came to console their sister. "It's okay, we got her now. Thanks," Tanya said.

As the sirens got closer, I told Muévete, "Superhero rule number one: when you defeat your enemies, make sure they're okay. They are still people, too. Rule number two: when you hear the cops coming, leave. Rule number three: after a long fight, get ice cream."

"Why ice cream?" she asked.

"Why not?" I said.

She smiled. Gave me a fist bump, and said, "Move" at herself and floated into the sky. I proudly flew by her side.

26

The next day, school was closed. There were obviously some major clean-up and repairs needed in the gym, water supply system, and football field. I can only imagine the look on Mr. Bookman's face when he saw the mess we caused.

Maya and Ronald came over to my house to hang out for the day. We watched the news to hear what the broadcasters had to say about the incident. Tracy was being interviewed but had very few answers. She really didn't remember much of what had happened. Last thing she said she remembered was that she was watching Mr. Bookman and the mop boogieing, and then she woke up covered in red paint on the football field with the Supadupa Kid and some 'strange girl' wearing a mask.

"'Strange girl!?' Tracy has a lot of nerve calling me strange! With that mask she was wearing, she looked like the Hunchback of Notre Dame!" Maya said while shaking her fist at the TV.

"Easy, Maya. We came out on top. No one got hurt, and no one knows that we are the good guys!" Ronald said triumphantly.

"Good guys and good girl!" Maya stated with confidence.

"Well, great job, team. Let's have a little fun since we have a day off from school. Wanna shoot some hoops? Play video games, or how about a board game?"

Both Maya and Ronald voted for a board game. We decided on the game Trouble, which was very fitting. We each picked a color, then I asked "Who wants to go first?" and Maya said, "I always MOVE first." We all busted out laughing. I bet you can figure out who won.

THE END
...for now!

**Follow Ty Allan Jackson on
all social media platforms
for information about
The Supadupa Kid, Danny
Dollar and everything in
the TAJ universe !**

About The Author

Ty Allan Jackson is an award-winning children's book author, youth motivational speaker, and literacy advocate. A three-time TedX presenter, Ty travels around the country inspiring children to read and educating adults about the impacts of illiteracy. Ty's books have been featured on CNN, NBC Nightly News, The Steve Harvey Show, PBS and the Hallmark Channel. He recently appeared on Marvel's Hero Project on Disney+ featuring Sydney Keys, a young man who was inspired by Ty's book Danny Dollar Millionaire Extraordinaire to create an innovative book club for African-American boys called BooksNBros. Ty is the co-founder of the Read or Else movement and the financial literacy program Danny Dollar Academy.

About The Illustrator

Jonathan Shears, born and raised in Adams, a small town in the Berkshires of Massachusetts, Jonathan spent most of his childhood designing countless original characters and cartoons. He graduated college with a Bachelor's degree in Media Arts & Animation from The New England Institute of Art. He later narrowed his focus on visual and interface design, as well as branding and identity. Currently, he lives in New Hampshire with his wife where he continues to create and use his imagination.

162

ACKNOWLEDGEMENTS

I'd like to give a big shoutout to the loves of my life Martique, Aja, Ajayi and Alia Jackson.

Also much love to Diane Brown, James Jackson, Manzo Jackson, Jasmine Jamison, Jermaine Foster, Everett Waters, Quentin Guerrero, The Fleming Family, Earl, Evelyn and Francisco Taylor, Denise Mediavilla, Rachel Malley, Nyna and Bob Malley, Jordan Diez, Jack Malley-Diez, Scott Moore, LaVaughn Davies, Nicole Davies, Jimmy Hall, The Dews Family, The Taylor Family, The Bissell Family, Noëlle Santos, Julie Boyd and Barrington Stage, The Red Book Shelf, The United Way, Peter Gannon, Jake McCandless and the world's greatest illustrator Jon Shears.

And a special acknowledgment to Javon Williams and the Williams family for providing the inspiration to SDK <3